WHAT HAPPENS IN NEBRASKA

WHAT HAPPENS IN NEBRASKA

POEMS

CAT DIXON

STEPHEN F. AUSTIN STATE UNIVERSITY PRESS

Production Manager: Kimberly Verhines
Cover Art: Rachel Brodsky

IBSN: 978-1-62288-933-4

For more information:
Stephen F. Austin State University Press
P.O. Box 13007 SFA Station
Nacogdoches, Texas 75962
sfapress@sfasu.edu
www.sfasu.edu/sfapress
936-468-1078

Distributed by Texas A&M University Press Consortium
www.tamupress.com

ACKNOWLEDGMENTS

"An Attempt at Collaboration" *Still: The Journal.*

"After Playing Minecraft, I Reflect on Love" *Whale Road Review.*

"Baryogenesis" *armarolla: a cabinet of literary curiosities.*

"Clouds" *Anti-Heroin Chic.*

"Denver to Colorado" *Gastropoda Literary Magazine.*

"The Distance" *Abyss & Apex.*

"The Ex-Boyfriend Returns to America" *Rat's Ass Review.*

"First drafts should be handwritten, He advises" *Lowestoft Chronicle.*

"He says, 'We had a falling out'" *Punch Drunk Press.*

"Horror Movie" *Bengaluru Review.*

"Keep Your Options Open" *Landlocked Magazine.* (Options 1-12)

"The Late Christmas Package," *Bengaluru Review.* (Option 13 in the poem "Keep Your Options Open")

"Letter for Your 47th Birthday" *Inquietudes Literary Journal.* (Titled "November")

"The Lighthouse" *13th Floor Magazine.*

"Meeting the Ex-Boyfriend on the 3rd Floor of the University Library" *SWWIM Every Day.*

"Messages" *Goat's Milk Magazine.*

"Meteorology" *Goat's Milk Magazine.*

"Midnight at the Keyboard" *Panoplyzine: A Literary Zine.*

"Minot" *Rat's Ass Review.*

"Missed Connection" *Eclectica Magazine.*

"My Friend and I Visit a Candy Store at 8:55pm on Tuesday" *Turnpike Magazine.*

"My lover has left, and everything is worse now" *Coastal Shelf.*

"Our Last Date" *Derailleur Press.*

"Patience" *Bengaluru Review.*

"Planted in My Backyard" *Young Ravens Literary Review.*

"Reflection on the Final Year" *IthacaLit: A Journal of Literature & Arts.*

"Relationships" *SWWIM Every Day.*

"Revising Poems with an Ex-Boyfriend" *Philosophical Idiot.*

"Shopping at Target with My ~~Ex-Lover~~ Friend" *X-R-A-Y Literary Magazine.*

"Sign Here" *Corvus Review.*

"Space Exploration" *They Said: An Anthology of Contemporary Collaborative Writing. Black Lawrence Press.*

"Summer 2008" *Dämfino.*
"Sunk" *Goat's Milk Magazine.*
"Sunday Morning" *Pidgeonholes Magazine.*
"Telescope" *The Bosphorus Review of Books.*
"Thank you for asking me" *Pidgeonholes Magazine.*
"To a Christian Man" *Thin Air.*
"The Unexpected" *Wimpole Street Gazette.* (Titled "Sail")
"What Happens in Nebraska," *Duende Literary.*
"What Happens to the Heart" *Still: The Journal.*
"When I Find the Miracle" *Duende Literary.*
"Wrestle with your own demons" *Rogue Agent.*
"You Can't Teach an Old Dog New Tricks" *Rat's Ass Review.*

CONTENTS

PART 1: IF YOU LEAVE, DON'T LEAVE NOW

My lover has left, and everything is worse now ⌒ 15

Missed Connection ⌒ 17

Midnight at the Keyboard ⌒ 20

"First drafts should be handwritten," he advised ⌒ 22

Telescope ⌒ 23

He says, "We had a falling out." ⌒ 24

Let the Stars Guide Us ⌒ 25

An Attempt at Collaboration ⌒ 26

Minot ⌒ 27

A Toast ⌒ 28

Sail ⌒ 29

He asks, "Can you describe it?" ⌒ 30

Baryogenesis ⌒ 31

You Can't Teach an Old Dog New Tricks ⌒ 32

The Distance ⌒ 33

Space Exploration ⌒ 34

Eventually ⌒ 35

The Ex-Boyfriend Returns to America ⌒ 36

Keep Your Options Open ⌒ 37

Sign Here ⌒ 42

PART 2: WE'VE ALWAYS HAD TIME ON OUR SIDE

Denver to Omaha ⌒ 45

Clouds ⌒ 47

Meeting the Ex-Boyfriend on the 3rd Floor of the University Library ⌒ 48

The Lighthouse ⌒ 50

Sunk ⌒ 51

If I Didn't ⌒ 52

Summer 2008 ⌒ 53

Relationships ⌒ 54

"Put your love to the test" ☞ 55

To a Christian Man ☞ 56

Patience ☞ 57

Sunday Morning in Potter, Nebraska ☞ 58

"Wrestle with your own demons" ☞ 59

What Happens to the Heart ☞ 64

Revising Poems with the Ex-Boyfriend ☞ 65

How to Loosen a Jar ☞ 66

Meteorology ☞ 67

The Stories of Shel Silverstein ☞ 68

PART 3: YOU ALWAYS SAID WE'D MEET AGAIN

What Happens in Nebraska ☞ 71

Our Last Date ☞ 73

The Ex-Boyfriend Moves Again ☞ 74

When I Find the Miracle ☞ 75

In the Loess Hills ☞ 77

This is not a tale ☞ 78

Planted in My Backyard ☞ 79

Horror Movie ☞ 80

To Get to the Other Side ☞ 81

Messages ☞ 82

Thank you for asking me ☞ 83

My Friend and I Visit Hollywood Candy at 8:55PM on a Tuesday ☞ 84

November ☞ 85

Reflection on the Final Year ☞ 87

Space makes ☞ 88

The First Meeting ☞ 89

Shopping at Target with My ~~Ex-Lover~~ Friend ☞ 90

New Year's Eve Message ☞ 92

After Playing Minecraft for the First Time, I Reflect on Love ☞ 94

WHAT HAPPENS IN NEBRASKA

PART 1: IF YOU LEAVE, DON'T LEAVE NOW

worse than the black hole that birthed me,
and then vacuumed the stars like dust,
the redshift that dims the eye, the coronagraph
with the moon of his mouth as its disk,
the payload door left open the entire flight,
the broken piece of cold metal
adhering without a scar;

worse than the duel at dawn with pistols drawn,
the arrow with its sturdy spine that pierces
the palm, the shattered shiny glass swept
into the dustpan, and washed down
the sink, the bite marks on the neck
after the struggle;

worse than the flourish of the ancient organ,
the dusty empty pews echoing silence,
some significance pinned to a wrinkled lapel
like a corsage, the sunrays rainbowing through
stained glass, the crucifix on the altar,
the baptismal font with its algae, the genuflection
of the elder knee;

worse than the man who holds the door
open and shakes my hand, the small
kindnesses of strangers—smile, nod, wave;
worse than the chirp of hello
that guts me;

worse than the frigid waters of the deep,
the sagging yellow lifeboat filled

with microscopic holes.
I was prepared to drown. I was not
ready for the sudden realization
that I could swim, and swim very well,
and that we were drowning together
of our own freewill.

MISSED CONNECTION

You're planning to move again,
 and you know I can't follow—

cuffed by mortgage, children,
and place devotion. Too many years

planted in the prairie—I tear up
at Omaha's skyline appearing as a mirage

in the sea of corn, blooming from I-80's cement,
as I race home after dropping off the kids

to their father's in the east for the summer.
Can we even call those short buildings

a skyline? Well, I do. Over the Missouri
the walking bridge is lit up like the yellow

brick road that leads to my front door.
I only visit the bridge in July at night

when jumping seems like an option,
when you're hundreds of miles away—

not available to play lifeguard.
I wonder if you'll miss the Midwest,

Runza, Dairy Queen, and the rest.
Eppley Airfield is my favorite airport—

two concourses—A and B—with that
welcoming Omaha Steaks kiosk

as if air travel lends itself to meat, so I agree
to meet you there before your flight—

need to see you off this one last time.
Sitting at a table in Godfather's Pizza,

me with two slices, you sipping on a soda,
I ask questions. You offer few answers.

Finally, you give a clue, but overhead
a voice calls, *The TSA would like*

to remind you not to leave your bags
unattended. Meaningless warning.

Now it's time for you to go
through security—they need to x-ray

your bag, shoes, and chest. Maybe
there's a beating muscle under your shirt,

I can't be sure. We hug before you slip
into the line, and then I turn, go down

the escalator for I can't follow you to the gate.
I freeze my face until I'm in my car

in the dark of the parking garage.
You don't know that my heart

tags along in your suitcase. In the front
pocket, where you might have stuffed

a magazine or book, she waits. How
am I to know you'll lose your bag

in the Denver airport while studying
the new art exhibit. Denver, an alien

monstrosity, complete with ice skating rink,
miles and miles of distance to run

from one gate to the next. You miss
the connecting flight. Your bag is turned

in, but you failed to fill in the card latched
to its handle. There's no name, no number.

Your suitcase sits for months in lost and found
until donated to the local Goodwill.

MIDNIGHT AT THE KEYBOARD

"Tonight I can write the saddest lines"
—Pablo Neruda

Write for example, 'The stars ache to burn this planet,
scorch our flesh; a universal holocaust.'

The winking cursor another star with desire to destroy.

Exaggeration breeds self-pity. This face I must wear,
pock-marked and discolored, masks my words.

These words I type—meaningless symbols—
what does it matter what I write?

Write for example, 'The clouds hide the moon
and stars to protect humanity from their glare

as the red wine clouds my memory
and allows me to lie down.'

The mirror above my bed reflects the light
from the neighbor's patio—a star hovers

in its frame and no curtain can darken my room.
Tonight I can write the saddest lines.

Inebriated, I shatter the glass. The shards
display a solar system across the floor.

Instead of sweeping them up, I turn
to the keyboard to record the image,

to send the words to him. Then, I must
hit pause, hit mute. He doesn't wish to hear from me.

These messages passed through keys, wires,
servers, and patient clouds are all futile.

What does it matter that he never loved me?

"FIRST DRAFTS SHOULD BE HANDWRITTEN," HE ADVISED

The backspace button is stuck again probably from the latest soda spill.
The keyboard eats my letters—hungry for the taste of commas and apostrophes,
famished from the snap of the spacebar and the flicker of the cursor. The bang
of the printer as it comes to life—its mouth full of ink and its tray dusty
with remnants of card stock—jolts me from this free-writing. See, this computer
zaps the word "there" into "here." Nothing is ever sent or received—
the mailbox *is* an eternal pending folder. The network connection lost.
The router's on Mars, the modem's in my neighbor's mouth—that neighbor
who insisted he had to drive across the city during snowstorms
to search for stranded motorists as if no one owned
a cell phone. He carried a shovel, jumper cables, a notebook, and a pick-axe
in his backseat. See, the self-driving car will be
a reality thanks to people working at computers.

When the car screeches off the road due to ice, a distress signal will be sent.
The neighbor can finally stay home. I think I will miss the free
road—the empty threat that I could jump the curb or race down the one-way
street going the wrong direction. I like options. When the options menu
pops up on the computer, I try to understand why this mouse
must highlight everything. Some strange setting I have yet to discover.
I can never determine which option is best, so I leave it be, hit restart
over and over, and that's the burn, the cut cord, the short circuit. I can
never find a clean sheet of paper in the tray, or erase the words I've spoken
instead of typed, or stop Gmail from predicting my words with auto-fill
as I type a message to him—I'm too lazy and will allow A.I. to finish.

TELESCOPE

This poem is a lens, no,
a mirror with its tarnished corners
and cracked edge. Each letter
I've scribbled blurs—speckled
gray. The words fluctuate.

On first read, the last
line ends in *love*, later

      it's *hue*.   *Together* becomes

          tether.   *Splinter* fuzzes

                      into   *split*.

Attempt to scrub
the glass with your hot breath
and hand. Fog clouds the page
and (by mistake?) you erase
          a word there
              a line here,
and this is now found
poetry. Title and claim
it as your own.

HE SAYS, "WE HAD A FALLING OUT."

We climbed that tree in your backyard, held hands on the highest branch before it cracked and threw us to the leaf-littered grass.

The hull of the ship that carried us through the Arctic Circle was torn by a glacier; we spilled out to the sea.

The surge of adrenaline overtook us as we dove from the airplane, yet we pulled the parachutes opened as trained; a gust of wind sailed you across the state line.

Occupied with our trajectory, we neglected to properly close the hatch and the shuttle's door burst open; we floated into the vacuum to join the stars.

LET THE STARS GUIDE US

We arrive to the table with such
different takes—your plans proclaim shoot straight
south until you're facing where rock touches
the Drake Passage and high winds and fate
slap cheeks red. I recommend a northern
path—let the stars guide us through frigid air
to a campfire. I'll bring all these poems to burn,
and you, packed so lightly without a care,
can school me on navigation, hourglass
dolphins, the speed of Earth's spinning axis.
The curling sparks of my words assign tasks—
stay, cleave, commit, flee. Frozen in paralysis,
you, a green-eyed snowman sailing by Cape Horn,
wink, but I'm too far away. The lines are torn.

An Attempt at Collaboration

The writing back and forth kept
the flame burning and while
it's nice to sit around a campfire,
char marshmallows, tell ghost stories,
and warm up your hands on cold nights,
it's not pleasant to be burned—skin scarred and sore.
This fire is one-sided, I always figured, but to keep
a torch going for over a decade is excessive.

When we began, I focused on using the terms
"persona" and "speaker" over the pronouns
"you" and "me," but as time passed, all
of the poems were embers and you wore
thick gloves for protection. My hands were bare.
I moved these sticks without concern
until it was too late. I can't keep at this—
my face, caked in ash and grit,
and my fingers, burnt black, flake off.

MINOT

Because it's cold,
he said, we should
camp in his cabin.

He had one chair, one
spoon, one bowl. Two
rooms were filled with

books and unopened
envelopes which he used
as scratch paper:

groceries lists, knock-knock
jokes, lines of poetry,
soup recipes.

He hogged the blankets
at night, napped incessantly
throughout the day,

and wouldn't kiss
on the lips. Yet,
his riddles, spicy

to the tongue, kept
me parched. His poems,
which I thought

he wrote for me, kept
me intrigued. In the dark
we held hands.

Huddled in front
of the wood stove,
I was sure we'd never

go hungry or get bored.
Snow kept him in,
but love drove me out.

A TOAST

Cheers to your bachelorhood—
guzzle oil from barrels while I sip
fresh water from a Hydroflask.
Cheers to your freedom—
crawl in scorched cornfields to hunt
mice while I, hunkered in my bunker,
dine on tender filet mignon topped
with mushroom sauce.
Cheers to your journey—
suffocate in 130-degree heat—
the horizon: smoky ash, the rain:
black ink. Here I sail on
the murky waters of abstinence.

SAIL

We have lingered long enough on the shores of the cosmic ocean.
We are ready at last to set sail for the stars.
—Carl Sagan

A fireball of hot gas flashed when
Shoemaker hit Jovian atmosphere
leaving black scars three times earth's size.

Some comets lose their way,
but don't focus on unplanned collisions.
Every violent impact schools us.

If you analyze everything,
meteors destined to pockmark
your lineage will paralyze you.

Like Rhea, we must save our sons,
replacing flesh for rock. Then water
them with a frequent *attaboy.*

I tire of this game, and I'd like
to hit the reset button.
I'd choose another character to play,
another realm to journey,
a different monster to defeat.

HE ASKS, "CAN YOU DESCRIBE IT?"

I'd say it's a parasite—a tick with thick
armor, the size of a housecat, and it carries
something stronger than Lyme Disease,
something that thrives off
the aloofness you water with riddles
and rhymes—this rash brings joint pain,
fever, fatigue. Like you, I imagine
it hatched from an asteroid, and feeds
off the blood of anyone close enough to love.

BARYOGENESIS

In the beginning was the heavy quark, and then there was you—bones, ligaments, eyes. Years later, I spied your maneuvers from my telescope. Like all those atoms hiding in galaxy clouds and floating out of sight, you gathered every piece of yourself and disappeared, but I kept up the search.

Like the dedicated astronomer, I chart each place—room 218, Dodge Street, that historical church where we held hands in the back pew—wherever I had kissed you needs to be observed. The scientists report that atoms hide in dark matter, so I brush my black strands, comb my pubic hair, and slit the side of these black tights and knee-high boots alone in my bedroom. In the corner of my field of vision, I catch a glimpse of a shadow slipping into the closet. If I pursue with this hunger, I know you'll dodge my mouth, my hands. Instead, I crawl to the door frame and finally my vigilance pays off. You've been tucked behind my dresses and shirts—all black—and you wear the bruises—black and blue—of a man on the run, an atom caught in ionized gas—always present, invisible to the naked eye.

A dozen times he emails asking
how to close a Google Doc. A hundred
texts ping with worry that his changes
are unsaved. All attempts
to train via phone and email
are in vain, and lightning
must flash in my word choice
or punctuation for he knows
I'm annoyed. I should shower
him with respect—the only thing a man
wants. Awkward with Google Docs,
nervous about the drive, he demands we
empty the cloud—now. His words may be
plagiarized, or god forbid read. Text
in this drive is set for our eyes only,
but he insists. Does he imagine
all those words raining
from cloud to hard disk? Do clouds
this dense even exist? Does he
believe that I would erase all this?
I click the icon of the two little gray
people. His role is editor. I hit "remove."
I say the drive is empty, but that's
another lie. Our words
will go unpublished, but not unheard.

THE DISTANCE

The rockets, like shooting stars,
zip across the sky and the red glare

will leave its imprint on your eye,
but take heart, for once they disappear,

their trails replaced with blue, you will
realize this longing isn't your fault—

you, stranded on earth with oil for water
and drone bees to pollinate the new crop

of strawberries, with balding patches
on the crown of your head and skin tags

dangling like price tags from your arms
and neck, surrounded by the vultures

of heat and dehydration, collapsing
onto a beanbag chair filled with ashes

and sand, relax. I have left you in this
dusty wasteland and now you are free

to repopulate and evaluate everything.

SPACE EXPLORATION

How can we invite space exploration
when we haven't discovered all there
is here? The ice crawlers in the glaciers,
the frilled shark swimming 5,000 feet
below the glimmer of the Pacific,
the palpitations of my heart when
we touch.

EVENTUALLY

Tell me again about her hair—dark, curly, and long, or how she brushes her fingers against your arm to steer you in the crowded market, or how her eyes are so bright that on the rocking bus ride up the mountain late at night you can read the map from their glow, or how she teases you about your accent, your clothes, or how she's thin—her doll-size wrists flail while rapidly speaking of her undone chores. Or tell me how you inch toward the wall when she stands too close, or how you step sideways in the doorway to avoid touching her shoulder, or how you hold your breath as to not inhale her soap when you must sit together in the back of her brother's car.

Tell me about her parents' farm—the chickens and rooster all flocking to the gate, lined up as if they know their fate, and they greet it warmly. We must entertain that eventuality. We must stare at one another, flapping our hands in excited speech recalling our feats and failures on some pasture not too far from here. Tell me you will wait for me to arrive and she will no longer be there. Tell me she's not real.

THE EX-BOYFRIEND RETURNS TO AMERICA

His arm hair curls up his wrist
to crooked knuckles. As he
slips my panties to my knees,
his thumb and index finger
press against my sweaty clit,
a bloated pineapple slice.

The Chilean maid, who kept
his house and ironed his shirts
for three years, then climbed in bed,
tasted like caramel and sweet
onion. *Why did you go in*
search of plums and peaches
in foreign countries? I ask.

Flicking his eyes to mine, he
inches his mouth from my thighs
and says with wet lips, I ate
star fruit every morning. At
night, I wrote verbose emails
to you that I couldn't send
due to spotty internet.

KEEP YOUR OPTIONS OPEN

Option 1

We meet at Runza. Perfectly compatible, we never argue. Perfectly organized, we never forget an appointment, a birthday, or what the other prefers. Perfectly healthy, we never grow old, get sick, or die.

This has never been an option. If you're that naïve, you might as well forget how to read.

Option 2

We meet at Caffeine Dreams. All in black, I sip hot chocolate and critique your words to avoid your eyes. The table's rickety and the tapping of keyboards at nearby clustered writing groups is as loud as seagulls, but this remains the best lifeboat for a woman who cannot float—a woman who would drink salt water despite the promise of increased thirst.

If you take a sip, see below. If you'd rather swim, go to Option 7.

Option 3

I invite you over for drinks and we talk for hours. If you choose to spend the night on the couch, go to Option 5. If you run to your rusted-out Ford parked down the street for fear of the wolf and his roar, keep reading.

In my den, I placed a writing desk in the corner, and on that desk I've lined up sleek pens from Korea. They look like long silver bullets in rows and keep the wolf at bay. Above the desk, a sign: CREATE. In red ink you mark up my stanzas. In blood I blot out every insult not delivered. No matter how fast you flee, the first three letters of my name written in cursive are strung together— that silken thread around your throat tightens as you stand on the office chair.

Hours later, I'm mesmerized by how you chomp on the bit I've placed in your mouth, stomp in a circle with that rope slicing into your ankle, scratch at your skin, howl. I lurk in the door ready to engage but think now is not the time. If I threw a tantrum like this, the wolf would label me immature and selfish. Start over or go to Option 6.

Option 4

We meet again in the psychology section of the university library. I invite you over for dinner—five people on the back deck. With a paper sack on your head and holding up a bag of corn chips, you pose for a snapshot next to the grill. The paper plates stacked up like stone tablets record the meal and command you cut the tomatoes, shuck the corn, and warm up the meat. The sudden downpour soaks us all.

If you find me attractive, finish the meal.

Option 5

You lie on the couch for an hour until I come take your hand. If you choose to sleep in my king-size bed and rummage through the room while I shower the next morning, you will discover in the bottom drawer of the dresser, I've hidden the New Testament. When the wolf attacks, I lock the bedroom door to read Matthew, chapters six and seven, and weep. There are no atheists inside a man's fist. I never purr amen after a prayer. I'm not that weak, yet I prayed for this.

I beg you not to leave while my wet hair dribbles down my back. The sliding glass door, which doesn't lock, counts every exit. I have forgotten the wolf's name, all the huffing and puffing. Let's pack a picnic basket with two oranges, cotton candy grapes, a loaf of French bread, and pinot. I will forget the bottle opener—I always disappoint.

Option 6

We meet at the blood bank on 38th and Dodge. I'm not allowed to give blood so I wait on the front steps for my ride. You appear with a band-aid and a chocolate chip cookie. I haven't seen a cassette in ten or fifteen years, but there you are with a Walkman and headphones. I stop myself from asking what you're listening to. You ask why I haven't donated. I lift up my sleeves to expose all those pretty white closed eyelids on my forearms. Guess my blood is tainted. Keep reading if you take a seat despite the July heat, the stares from strangers heading to their cars, the bus you intend to take home rolling up.

We complain of Dodge Street—with its complicated rules (you can't turn right!) (this lane goes west now; east later)—the main artery in Omaha. If traffic stops here, it backs up everywhere, so the city constructs an overpriced, overhead massive beltway to ease the flow, and still with everyone going west at 5pm, there's an accident every day, every rush hour, a delay. See, all men eventually go west. You go west and I hitchhike to another blood bank that will reject me just like the rest. Next.

Option 7

At the city pool, I lounge in a chair under an umbrella. Fear of water prevents me from entering even the shallow end. You lap the pool for an hour and leave without saying goodbye despite my rubbing sunscreen on my spread thighs, the grapes I kiss into my mouth each time you turn my way, my weak waves. Weeks later, you still won't return my calls. I imagine you jogging past my house with your Walkman or swimming at the man-made lake down the street. Surrounded by cement and water, I sink. Your cassette tape with its reel pulled out—a black rosary wrapped around your finger—is a noose on both of our necks dragging us back to something we missed. If you call again, go to Option 11. If you don't, continue to Option 12.

Option 8

Location doesn't matter—the weather does. Rain says we'll make it. Sun and blue sky, a backdrop to our missed connection. Snow and ice go either way. I can't predict your route, your reaction. Exhausted from the hunt, I pour a glass of wine and recline in bed. See, the wolf preys at night in any season. When he shatters the sliding glass door and stalks to my room, I don't hide in the closet where every dress lies on the floor where it fell. Later, I don't cry over the wounds. Here in this pink nightgown floating on these damp sheets, I must appear threatening for I invite you over every day, but something keeps you at bay—perhaps the knotted webs in my tangled black hair, the yelp that escapes when you touch my leg, the gaping hole in my chest that mirrors hell. I want to imagine it's the storm clouds that keep you away. Isn't that just as well?

Option 9

We meet at the concession stand—you order a corndog and I ask if they have a meal for vegetarians. The state fair with its cotton candy, country music, and Ferris wheel attracts children, and I'm here playing widow with a niece and nephew. I thank you for the left-over tickets you offer.

Option 10

I haven't left the house much except for vodka and cigarettes runs, but my friend Joy insists I need words, so we arrive at The Bookworm, to hear you read from your first collection. Joy and I purchase copies and we get in line to have them signed. You ask her name, scrawl *all the best* on the inside cover, and ask if she's a writer. Joy, now overjoyed, gushes about her cow poems. The cover of your book displays knots—slippery hitch, artificial eye, shroud, but upon reading, I find no rope in the lines. Still, I send an email to invite you to my workshop group that hasn't met in months.

If you come to the meeting, go back to Option 2.

Option 11

I meet another man and stop listening for the phone. He shaves his head, burns poems into wood tablets—the wood painted black, the words, red, and when I invite him to my bed, he pounces—faster than the wolf which still prowls the perimeter of my yard, hungrier than the fire in the swollen pit where all promises turn to ash and ride the wind—and I, never left alone, have no time to return your long email apologizing for the delay. You hit refresh over and over waiting for my reply. If you want me to reconsider, you must drown your pride, burn your name into my lawn, and shoot the wolf with a silver bullet.

Option 12

You enter the waiting room of a therapist's office. I nod, pick up a magazine, and flip through the pages while examining your every move. I want to ask you what you're doing here. I want you to ask why I've settled so I can shrug as if it doesn't matter. You sit, stretch your legs, and your black work boot hits the coffee table. The vase tips and before it can spill its red petals, cloudy water, and pink pebbles, you catch it with your hand, easing it to stand again. The water droplets that soak into the rug spell out *run*.

Option 13

You wait at the post office for a package. The card left in your mailbox doesn't name the sender—you're curious. When you reach the counter, you're handed a box marked *delicate, fragile, handle with care* with no return address. Back at home you consider tearing it open; instead, you put it on the top of the fridge to collect dust. It may be a bomb and you haven't the nerve to open or even shake the box. You phone me later to ask if I have sent it, but my number has been disconnected. So, you send an email, but it bounces back. Your chest tightens, but you're not having a heart attack. All the wonderful things in this world are delivered lacking instructions.

SIGN HERE

Your signature is a tocsin of surrender—a white-out erasure. If you
take my banner, it'll stream behind you like a kite—it will pull you to the
edge. You're like the mascot at the street corner with the "going out of
business-everything half-off-everything must go" notice. You toss the sign,
catch it, slink it behind your back, flip it, and slide it between your legs—
always the showman. No, you're the torn flag that waves its shredded self
to no salute. No, you're the cataract that drifts by, a lazy swimmer back
floating, and with every blink or twitch, the dot dunks out of sight. I close
one eye awaiting your next appearance.

PART 2: WE'VE ALWAYS HAD TIME ON OUR SIDE

DENVER TO OMAHA

The 4pm take-off had been delayed because of ice on the wings—
freak October storm. Folks grumble. Flight attendants soothe
with Vodka and free pretzels and nuts. In seat 12B, I fidget
with my skirt, my hair, the handle of my purse, annoyed
with the bags of peanuts I classify as dangerous thanks
to my daughter's allergy, and even though she's not with me now,
the foil pops and crackles of those bags are like grenades
and land mines exploding. I open my carry-on at my feet
which holds books to read. I'd lugged all of this to the mountains
and now must lug it home. I fish out a new book, signed by the author
—a gift for you.

Twenty minutes into the flight, the cabin lights flicker. I count
the number of aisles to the nearest exit—portal to cloud,
snow, fog. *Just to be safe.* When the lights go out, a child whines.
When the plane hiccups, jostling stomachs and luggage, I wonder
why the floor illumination we were promised would light the way
during an emergency doesn't spark. I think of your hands
on my thighs in the dark, you whispering my name, your sharp scent
after a morning jog. "Oh, God, is this happening?" The lady behind
me cries. I brace my back, push into the seat: *become part of the plane,*
become part of the plane, a chant to drown out the passengers
—the rumbles of the engine.

The masks, demonstrated by the flight attendant as we waited
impatiently on the tarmac, do not fall; the flight attendant
does not call over the intercom or enter the cabin; the plane
does not level out. The nosedive rocks us to silence. One moment
you're in the air annoyed by a man crunching peanuts across the aisle;
the next, you're in a cradle in a treetop. The branch cracks.
Now the descent. The plummet to exit. Here is the screech
of metal—rows of seats crunching together like an accordion
and the roof scraping off like a lid from a can of corn. We spin

until finding rest here. Snowflakes fall from the sky, and I sit
at a bench in Elmwood Park.

I wait for my daughter to finish a snowman. I promise
hot chocolate with her blanket warm from the dryer once
we return home. I raise my right hand covered with blood and snow.
This is not Omaha. This is not a park. The little girl with her white coat
disappears into a drift. I can't move to dig her out of the abyss, and you
will not save us for you escaped years ago.

CLOUDS

1.
The clouds overhead flank
a spine that spirals across the blue.
Is that your x-ray displayed
to signify the ultimate sacrifice?

2.
The splintered half-lines are branches
of my moist bronchial tree
swelling with the setting sun,
bursting with yellow birds in flight.

3.
The bones belong to the fish
that swims parallel to the halo
crowning your head, to the long curl
of your calf as you glide to the right.

4.
Adam's ribs are here to rank. See,
I was formed from man—crafted
from a roll of dice—rushing to bone,
returning to dust, hanging by the string of a kite.

MEETING THE EX-BOYFRIEND ON THE 3RD FLOOR OF THE UNIVERSITY LIBRARY

I.
This is the quiet section, so we whisper as we sort—
my pile has 50 poems. Yours, 30. With a red pen,

you slash through entire stanzas, draw arrows—
move this here, move that there. You say my line

must bait the hook for the next. Each piece
is tethered by the invisible push and pull

of the current. This table, floating in the corner
with a view of the parking lot, now spins,

caught in a whirlpool. I get seasick easily,
but you, chewing on a pen cap, shuffling

manila folders, do not seem to mind the spray
of the water, the carousel of silver sharks,

the dented eel that slithers in my lap,
the shaky hand I use to take notes.

II.
It seemed like a good idea all those years ago,
to salvage our lost letters, poems, and emails

to construct a lifeboat. All that wasted
time and emotion put to use—to make

something to pass the hours, something
to busy our minds, something

so lopsided and ugly that it would
never carry its passengers to shore.

The anchor latched to my broken ankle
guarantees I'll be pulled under,

and you, forever captain, former martyr,
the hero hidden in every book,

are destined for the lighthouse.
Just a little farther.

III.
On my laptop, I create a Google Drive—
organization will be so much easier.

We cut and paste and insert a new page break,
but the words smear the screen, my backspace

button gets stuck with seaweed. You
insist we work on paper. Forget

the computer, the cloud that holds
the secret of what happened to the sailor

who didn't drown, didn't abandon
ship, didn't kiss my mouth, and then spit

seashells in my face. His siren call
keeps the rain away, plugs the holes,

and I believe I can hold my breath
for as long as it takes.

THE LIGHTHOUSE

You abandoned
our sinking ship,
and then swam
to shore to face
the dark waves
crashing against
the rock, to taste
the spray as it
sprinkled the coast,
to hear the haunting
siren's call, to climb
the winding
stairs to perch
on the ledge—
100 feet high.
My raft was about
to ram the rocks,
but you refused
to flash the light
or call out a warning.
This is how love
always ends—one left
to drown, one safe
on shore, and the sky
filled with a million
witnesses to the gore.

SUNK

It was deemed necessary
to evacuate the submarine—
oxygen levels low and water
flowed through the vents.

Legends of ghost ships with ghost mates
circulated—men who hunkered in the head,
munching tangerines as they flipped through
ream after ream of blank saturated
pages as if reading magazines.

Our motley crew caught without a ship,
from a distance, looked like
little dots keen for water—fish
fighting the net, the hook, the land.

What we sought in the waves had
rusted and sunk. What we found
inside of each was rot. I wished
for a massive yacht—sails that touch
the sky—eighty meters long with
an inflated lifeboat like a tumor at its side.

When we arrived at the hotel, we were given the handicap accessible room complete with the large shower in the bathroom featuring a spray hose, plastic seat and railing. Did I ask you to shower with me? If I did, you said no. If I didn't, I wasn't ready for the rejection.

When we entered the party hours earlier, poets drunk on the patio, books scattered across tables, people assumed we were a couple. We sailed the rooms and left a wake like the train on a wedding dress. Did I ever ask you? If I did, you said no. If I didn't, my mouth was full of salt and sand.

When we talked about my near-drowning twenty years ago, you offered to teach me to swim and said you used to be on the high school swim team. Did I ever ask to set a date to meet at the local pool? If I did, you said no. If I didn't, I wanted to drown.

When the water fills my lungs and my hair spreads out like ink on the surface, will I reach my hand up? Will I struggle? If I do, will you throw me a life preserver? If I don't, will you jump into the cold, dark lake? Or will you turn, sprint to the car, rev the engine, and burn rubber?

It was the summer of impromptu invitations to coffeeshops, Shakespeare on the green, and moon-gazing. The heat intensified—birdbath water boiled, sweat pooled in lounge chairs, and dogs no longer barked even when the sun set. The neighborhood was silent.

It sounds—or the dearth of sound sounds—like you're not interested

Carrying a baby on my hip while I chased a toddler, I chased you— emails, phone calls, and texts. No matter how many words I wrote, you remained oblivious. I blamed the heat. No. I blamed the children. No man wants another's burdens, and no one would fault you. It's quite the feat to run a marathon with 50 pounds on your back in 100-degree heat. When a door creaks and opens to a brown lawn, the man will exit without a word.

I have memorized this book and own more copies than anyone. Yet you would not leave me with a cliffhanger, or begin this love story in medias res. You follow the arc, predictable and honest. In hot showers, I close my eyes and flash back.

I won't mention it again lest I sound like I'm pestering you and you write a blistering poem about me

You are a blister that electrifies every step, but no one would fault you. When a woman chooses to live in proximity to a volcano and go barefoot through lava flows, she knows the risk.

RELATIONSHIPS

It's night on a gravel road—the dead-end sign lit up by headlights, so I throw that mother into reverse. The tires squeal as I hit pavement yanking the wheel to find another street. Every light is green so I accelerate—what else can I do?—racing to the next stop. When the light flashes yellow, I don't slow down—time is short—I have to make it. I drive seven years straight. When the sun sets, the headlights from other cars blind so I look to the yellow line on the side of the road and follow it—an arrow pointing to the next house I will call home. When I enter, I know the place—black leather couch, dusty bookshelves, kitchen counters lined with empty water bottles and I set to work—polish, wipe, recycle—a mindless charade. When he walks in the door, I call him the wrong name. Who could blame me? They all look the same. Another fight over the car keys—my arm left aching from his grasp—another chance to be in the driver's seat. Back on the road, I brake at the stop sign, stare in my rearview, and head for the well-lit taxi stand at the airport. I hop in the cab, shout "drive," and he merges into traffic—just another pair of eyes shining into the night.

"PUT YOUR LOVE TO THE TEST"

I was raised in the 80s on soap operas, Happy Meals, and Madonna.
So, I stood there with a recalled Ruger demanding proof.
With your hands tied behind your back,
your feet bound to the chair, you maundered.
I duct taped your mouth. No more riddles.
No more tales. Those soap writers had lied:
people don't gush their feelings.
When the gun fell to the ground,
it fired into the writing desk. The bullet
buried, a hidden treasure, I would've asked you
to collect, but you weren't in that room.
You never came to visit.
That rickety chair and insanity were reserved
with ample time and no witness—
the rope around my neck,
the Ruger to my temple,
my cold meal uneaten on the table.

TO A CHRISTIAN MAN

I write to you.
I shouldn't be. Divorced, dirty atheist,
I'd never get a second look,
but what if I color my hair, change my name
to Mary Magdalene, you call yourself Jesus,
and we'll go away from here and make
things appear where nothing was,
multiply like fish and loaves of bread?
What would Jesus do if a pretty, little thing
like me sat on his lap? By myself
I could raise Lazarus and the church.

By myself, I twist my curls and each knot
becomes a thorn. I brush
my hair for weeks waiting for a reply.

PATIENCE

I'm going to sit here until you lick my fingers,
trim my nails, and then offer to paint them

—gray or pink—for you own the nail file
and have that bottle of polish poking out

your back pocket. I'll wait until you plunge
into my curly black hair, rub my forehead, get me

to purr like a cat, and you braid these wild waves
into a river down my back. Until you call out my name

like it's the *amen* at the end of a prayer, and finally stop
proselytizing, stop reciting the story of David,

and how all we need is a fast. Until you let me
feed you nachos covered in meat, cheese

and black olives, and the crunch of teeth annoys
me, and I know you're no longer hungry. Until you let me

remove my shirt, you put down that bag, and kneel
like a monk at a shrine. See here, see here,

I have lit all the candles and pulled out every tooth
just so I could display the universe on this church pew.

The front of the church is blank—no symbols on the walls,
no banners or signs. Love is an open room,

a sanctuary with the best acoustics. So when I say
those words, the robes and reserved signs will burn in the chalice

—that heavy, back-breaking pewter chalice—and its flame
will be visible blocks away. When the snake sparks and smokes,

everyone will be warmed, and now I'm eating your shed skin.
Ask, *where do I begin?*

SUNDAY MORNING IN POTTER, NEBRASKA

In your car leaving the small Baptist church,
you in tie and suit, me in my short blue dress,
you asked what I thought of the sermon.
I braided my hair, said how we were the most
attractive people there, but you didn't agree.
You persisted until I lamented the hymns,
and you reached over to touch my thigh.
I brushed your hand away. The car disappeared,
so did the scowl, and I was propelling
down I-80 in a van with Holloway and Sean—
racing from Denny's for we couldn't pay
for that breakfast, and they kept passing the blunt
back and forth until they finally remembered me
in the backseat. Dizzy, I fell asleep. Minutes later,
I sat up straight and saw a semi with "England"
written on its back door, and I called out,
"How far have we've gone?"
They snickered and kept driving.
Because I wanted to wear that dress—
gotta dress up for church—I had shaved my legs,
and because I had shaved my legs so fast
without water or cream, they burned—raw and pink.

He says I shouldn't write
in persona. *Write about your own damn life.*
Without an escape, I've hidden
in my closet behind those long dresses
that cover my legs. No one searched for me.

If he wants the truth, I spent
summers in a chair in Betty's house
for fourteen hours a day, seven
days a week. The walls and books
stained by cigarette smoke,
the grandfather clock chiming
every hour—its ticking ate
days and weeks. Betty snored
in her recliner so loudly
Barbara Walters on 20/20—
blond hair, sharp suit—was
voiceless. I tried to read her lips.
Mark, always in the corner
rocking and whispering, crawled
over and made eye contact for the first time—
how blue—and he pulled my hair.
Betty said the lamb on my hair tie
tempted his hands. At naptime,
I was next to Ashley who smelled
like plastic; her hair like pulled brown weeds.
Betty didn't bathe children,
but she did change Mark and Ashley's diapers.
She changed the other boy, 11 or 12
(I've forgotten his name),
who laid on the couch, never moving,
who had his feeding tube waiting
there like an empty vase for water and roses.

Ashley, with her balding head,
lowered ears, wide-set eyes, grabbed
my hand as we sat watching TV.
I jerked away and saw her wrist
was bruised—blue and green—
like a flower corsage given to a date
at prom or homecoming.
I won't write about the beatings.

See, I'm fishing and the wind
picks up and the sky's dark green.
This fish, detached from the hook,
wiggles and jerks. The scales slice
my fingers, and I let go. His body slaps
the wooden dock—

        he flips

                over   and   over.
      He plunges back into the lake.
      Just let that one go.

If he wants the truth, I was sent away at 18.
When that man washed his hands,
the hairs on the back of my neck
stood at attention—soldiers marching
the room into shock. The jolts sent
me into spasms, but I was strapped
down—the man refused
to let me leave. A flame tunneled
down my spine seeking the earth,
and like a charred tree, all
that remained was bark
and burnt leaves on the dirt.

      Lightning pock-marks my vision
      and mutes meaning. See, I bite
      my fingernails, drink too much wine,

vape on this nicotine stick,
obsess over Leonard Cohen, baseball legends,
Larry David, the space program, Bonhoeffer,
Seinfeld trivia, French cuisine, Medea,
the unattainable man, and Margaret Atwood
to avoid the tornado siren that blares.

When the tornado warning
was announced, I was in the library,
my second year of college, those
campus sirens screaming,
and the people, nameless and white,
all hollered   *stay here*   *stay here*
—I exited the front doors into the rain
and wind. I knew I couldn't die
for I had survived nights
filled with infanticide, and later,
the rage of lava. What could hail and
gales do to me that I hadn't already
weathered? What did it even matter?

I never learned how to ride a bike,
to skate, to jump rope, or swim.
The sky has always been the ceiling.
The ceiling fan always the sun.
While standing on a kitchen chair,
I jammed my finger up hoping to cut
off a digit—instead, a mouthful
of dust and spider web. Home was
salt and pepper shakers from every state,
miniature houses with tiny inviting
doors and windows, an unused
treadmill that was a coat rack,
and the never-silent TV. Tom Brokaw,
my father. Or maybe Regis Philbin.
My mother, Erica Kane,

a soap opera character that I watched
religiously in the summer. The bar
Tommy took me to after *All My Children*
was over, basted in overdone smoke,
but I liked the way the old stool spun
and the never-ending supply
of salty pretzels. Weekends
meant Tommy's grandchildren
visiting and holding me down
while she disappeared to smoke
and drink in the kitchen.

The truth is I found a book—
in Tommy or Betty's house,
not sure which—printed in 1923,
and its binding was worn, pages brittle,
and I brought it home, tucked in my pants,
and hid it beneath my bed. When my friend
Sheila spent the night, she lost a sock,
and found the book. I demanded she
drop it, but she held her side of the book
and would not let go. I grabbed and pulled.
Eventually it ripped. We each held half.
That night we snacked on candy
we stole from the kitchen while my mother slept.

Now, when the aging beast invites me
to dinner, I know I'm on the menu.
I can't resist. I drag my babies,
cowering and yawning,
to the table in a poorly lit room
so the beast may snap their necks, and leave.

>   See, the swaddling was too tight,
>   the arm of the rocking chair
>   too hard, the volcano
>   on the neighboring island—

a laboring cancerous lung—
polluted the air and dusted
my dark dresser and bed.
When we moved to Nebraska,
the furniture traveled along
with gritty Pacific salt embedded
in its grain. The lava spilled
from her mouth and I was
"idiot" "dipshit" "bitch"
and I carried those words
in my head until I discovered
releasing them felt better.
And better still, the vodka
on ice, a whole glass
filled to the brim. Black
out. That's where I've been.

The truth is the man the beast
chose to bring into our home
clawed at my thighs, chased me around
the house, and asked to give me
a "bath" instead of a "baby shower"
when I told them I was pregnant
with what he later called "bastard."
At eight months pregnant, the man
said I was so large I blocked out the sun.
At a restaurant, the man said to the waitress
my mother did not need dessert—*look at her.*

The truth is I've chosen not
to wrestle what I know I can never
defeat. Better to believe
a lie, make up this fantasy, than
to waste tears on the demons—
for they always return to the door,
always slip under the sheet,
always have the last word.

WHAT HAPPENS TO THE HEART

When you remove the bandage, don't be alarmed
by the bruise, blood, and stench. Covered things
tend to moisten, prune, and mold, and this
wound has festered for a decade. One can imagine
the infection and decay. Use the rubbing alcohol
left on the counter—note that the entire bottle is not enough.
The numbness dissipates and your skin burns. No
matter. This sensation does not faze you. Like words
and tears, nothing ignites reaction.

REVISING POEMS WITH THE EX-BOYFRIEND

You admit perhaps tinkering
with your lines, cutting aloof
excess, removing the mask
may be necessary. Plunge
beneath Cheyenne County's

soil, lather your burned shoulders
with gooey aloe vera,
uncoil the gray cord that bound
my wrists above my head, smash
your old fat laptop against
the headboard, and tell me, strong
grunting man, that words you sent
are like orgasms, fleeting.

HOW TO LOOSEN A JAR

At the restaurant, soda was served in lidless
Mason jars with paper straws. We sat staring
at the menus. I held many questions such as,
Who invented the Mason jar? You lectured
on thermal expansion: if a lid won't budge,
let hot water run over it. For ten minutes
you played the science teacher you once were,
and droned on until the waiter returned. With our
meals ordered, I redirected to the inventor,
but you didn't have the answer. You carried on:
your mother canned jams and jellies,
fruits and fruit juices, pickles and relishes.
When our food arrived, I asked
about us. Made of bleached glass,
the words were transparent. Everything
inside was on display, eager
for your taking. You listed off my mistakes.
I wanted to jot them on a napkin, to keep
that balled-up napkin in my pocket,
so I wouldn't forget again, but I didn't.
Later, I Googled Mason jar. The inventor
had been married with six daughters,
but you did have something in common:
Mr. Mason abandoned his work
before the design could really take off.

METEOROLOGY

Had I known the forecast,
or seen the clouds on the horizon,
I wouldn't have made contact.
I can't interpret radar. In school,
instead of science class, I weaved
worlds in a notebook where fear
reigned with its complicated
cues and insidious hunger
devouring all the paper.

He had spent time in the lab
with the Bunsen burner and beaker;
hours in the classroom studying air flow.
So when the moment came to experiment
and hypothesize, he had it pegged.
I had to learn the lesson there
—shoulder to shoulder. Had I known
the chemical clouds spewing
from the table meant indifference,
I wouldn't have stayed. Now
my taste buds are burnt off
 and at the sound of the word
"love," like him, I run.

An Amazon package arrives in December. Hardcover books for my kids.
The note: *Happy Holidays.*

The Missing Piece. I'm the missing piece that you grasped in your mouth,
neglecting self-preservation. We rolled one summer—over beds, the
golf course by Elmwood Park, hotel rooms—and then you spit me out
to search for what? Westward, Ho? Southern travel? The loneliness of
bachelorhood and the promise of an eternal life because you do not burn
like the church founders who died alone and penniless?

The Giving Tree. I'm the tree. You want shade? Here. You want my arms
tight around your neck embracing the smell of aloe vera and sweat? Here.
You want this trunk cut and etched with your poetry? Here. You want to
ship me out to sea, elongate your days and nights, and succumb to foreign
lands and pineapples? Here. Then you wander off. Finding no shelter, you
go to the desert.

This is a lovely book set, reiterating how I'm a mud-caked shoe left on
your patio after digging a ditch in a village all afternoon, then tossed—the
stench too strong to remove, so you find a cab to buy shoes at the market,
but you can't bargain in Spanish. You know *zapatos* and *dinero.* You—
encircled by banana trees and lonely women who stare at your green eyes,
grizzled face, lips that rhyme words in English—rest here.

PART 3: YOU ALWAYS SAID WE'D MEET AGAIN

WHAT HAPPENS IN NEBRASKA

Across the state—six hours with one stop for gas—
I raced, leaving behind the baby and toddler
with my soon-to-be-ex-husband, to visit Potter,
a Podunk town, one of the last stops before Nebraska
runs into the west. *Perhaps he'll let me stay.* We met
at Walmart at midnight. Exhausted, I wanted to cry,
to sleep, but he insisted on buying supplies for my five-day
stay: sunscreen, yogurt, orange juice, and vodka.

Two nights later, after dinner at the nicest restaurant in town,
30 miles from the Wyoming border, we sat under the stars.
Dizzy from the drinks, itchy from the chiggers, pressed into dirt,
I was dirt. Later, in his room, I was tied up
with the vacuum cleaner cord, my arms and legs
bound like a slab of cow at the slaughterhouse, a hanging
hunk of meat that would shiver and stale. Intoxicated,
I would've said *yes yes yes* to anything, but I would've
said yes in any state. No, that's a lie. All requests
were ignored. It was Labor Day weekend.

The next day he asked me to attend his church,
so I sported the red cuts on my wrists. I traced
and massaged the lines for attention. That's another lie.
I had no lines. I wouldn't sing the hymns, wouldn't say
amen, wouldn't pretend to be a virgin. It was over.
He had his God. I had these dusty trophies—
false memories, scars, and herpes.

In the spring we met in the middle at a Motel 6 in Kearney.
He pulled up our song on YouTube—laptop resting
on the bed—with no lyrics on the screen, he sang every word,
without hesitation. "If you leave… if you leave…
if you leave…" he crooned. Years later, I read

the lyrics off a website. *Why sing that to me?*
Was that goodbye? He must have forgotten
that I've kept every letter, email, text, poem,
and conversation tucked inside my pockets.
What would Jesus say about the moon, the pumpkin, the dog—
all metaphors for my heart that he pushed away?

Reader, if you visit me in Nebraska, I will share
the details of that evening in the motel and
what really happened that summer. He will say
he doesn't believe in censorship. *How dare anyone*
anywhere ban anything! Who dares question
a man's motives? He sends another email
from South America after finding my sixth
scandalous poem online. My black fan oscillates
like my moods—the whisper of its blades sing. I speak
his name, and here are titles for new poems I'll send to the wind:
tent, twenty, tenacity, trench, truth, trudge, truancy,
trend, rent, vent, fret. In Nebraska, I live alone.
He squats in the desert waiting for a reply.

OUR LAST DATE

In a crowded amusement park, in line for the barnyard bumper cars, we wait an hour, and as soon as the kid working the controls opens the little gate, you change your mind, grab my hand, and we go to the ice queen roller coaster. We're waiting in line here for two hours. Sweat dribbles down our backs. We don't talk—hypnotized by the three white carts that chug up the track, fall back down, and then start over. *I'm hungry.* So, we leave our spot and go to the popcorn stand. Ice cream is listed on the menu, but the worker dressed as a pig says he has none. Now you have a new mission. A parade starts down the mid-way. We flip-flop through strollers and mascots of cartoons I've never seen. You must have your ice cream. This is our only day here, tickets so expensive, and we will not return. We have yet to get on one ride.

Finally, two hours later, after we've eaten, after we've waited in three more lines, we sit in a gondola—its bottom attached to a track. We begin outside—I wave to the people still in line (*Look at us! We made it!*)—then our boat-for-two glides into a tunnel. A baby in another float down the line cries, hiccups, screams, and then a mother's shrieks echo—did she fumble? The water is dark green, gears hidden there just a few feet below. Every gondola jolts to a stop. A recorded voice repeats: *Mother Goose asks you to please stay in your seat.* The emergency lights are on now. The walls are black. Since we just entered, there's nothing to look at except each other and the murky water. An hour later, the boat jerks back to life and we pass Goldilocks and the three bears, Red Riding Hood discovering the wolf in grandmother's bed, the smart little pig peeking out the window of his brick house at the wolf slumped in defeat, Jack and Jill on top of a hill of flowers, yet the robots are not moving—frozen in mid-action—and all the yellow beam spotlights blind.

Out of the tunnel, the moon and stars glow, the crowd's smaller. You take my hand to help me off the boat once we reach the dock, and then we begin the long walk back to the parking lot. We don't stop to pick up a souvenir or hit the restroom one more time. Once out the gate, among the cars, we can't remember where we parked and search aimlessly. I asked for love in the boat, but you don't have it, so I'm off on an abandoned broom I found next to the Dumpster. I will find that candy house where a witch works with sugar and ovens to make magic.

THE EX-BOYFRIEND MOVES AGAIN

While you hauled boxes through freshly painted rooms and scrolled job listings
    on the net,
I called your disconnected number—a buzzing wasp trapped in the handset—
and fretted in my office chair with my fingers tangled in the long phone cord.
While you auctioned your childhood, future price, past doom,
I played Candy Crush and wasted at least $200 and thousands of hours.
While you wrote and submitted poems to dozens of journals,
I pandered holy trinkets wishing each customer was you in disguise.
While you shopped for bookshelves and new sheets and lamps,
I flirted with the orderlies in hopes I'd receive better treatment.
While you watched movies and read books and posted reviews on your blog,
I launched a hundred daydreams all ending with you knocking at my door
    carrying a suitcase and sporting a tie.

WHEN I FIND THE MIRACLE

After Leonard Cohen

Like a cough that interrupts a laugh,
Like a balloon popping in your hand,
Like a burn scarring skin pink and raw,
I leave a mark that fades.

Like an apple sliced in half,
Like an earthquake cracks the land,
Like a mirror steamed and fogged,
Show how you were made.

Like a cow nudges her new calf,
Like a diary makes no demands,
Like a razor dirty and dull,
If I have cut you, throw me away.

Like the current carries the raft,
Like the wind erodes the large dam,
Like a house with only three walls,
If I have disappointed, you must say.

Like a street with no streetlight,
Like a mean guitar with no strings,
Like a novel with its torn cover,
This is all you have paid.

Like a boxer with no fight,
Like a bird with a broken wing,
Like a mover with a frozen shoulder,
Our skin loosens and we age.

Like a tree clasping a lost kite,
Like a doorbell with a silent ding,
Like the aviary filled with feathers,
I simulate the better way.

Like a left-handed boy forced to write right,
Like the indentation from a lost ring,
Like the hip that predicts the weather,
If I whisper now what will you say?

IN THE LOESS HILLS

When the sugar clay moistens
with downpours and snow melts,
the soil loses all cohesion. Here,
thousands of years ago, glaciers grinded rock,
carving the earth. Today, with few clouds above,
an artist stands in the open front door
of a ranch house waiting for his father.
I glance out the bedroom window hoping
to catch a glimpse of god.

Both abandoned, but no longer alone,
together, we painted the house pink,
the chimney blue, the landscape
red, yellow and raw sienna. We planted
the trees, dyed the leaves green,
and shaded the shadows that fall
below the branches. When a man has
waited decades to be this free,
he is permitted to paint everything.

THIS IS NOT A TALE

The Glenwood acreage, in the hollow of the Loess Hills, was lonely with
its cracked front step, a spade and shovel lying on the overgrown sidewalk,
the rusted tractor beyond the barn, the tire swing with its frayed rope. The
property still boasted a bird orchestra at dawn, an insect serenade at dusk,
the neighbor's loose dogs prowling in the fields, the long gravel driveway,
your unseen midnight journey to the mailbox. There hidden in the rose
bushes was the house key, but when I snatched it midday, it didn't unlock
any of the doors, so I dug deep—borrowed the neighbor's overpowered
auger. Later, a team of squirrels completed the hole for the price of
roasted peanuts, carrots, and squash. Thirty feet below the petals, thorns,
and dirt, I found the reason my letters and knocks went unanswered. Here
in the bunker, a replica of the house, without windows or paint, you hid
from the meatpackers and the ghosts of the town's golf courses. Here,
on your typewriter you pecked away, suggesting that I come visit. Yet, I
found the bunker vacant. All the paper next to the desk was unused. All
the drawers and closets empty. The trash cans full of typewriter ribbons,
correction wheels and spools, and eraser shavings.

PLANTED IN MY BACKYARD

My dearest friend planted the seed years ago. The soil was rocky, the thorns of the rosebush threatening, yet he insisted he plant it *here*— claimed it was the most opportune spot. How could I have known that this tree would grow 12 feet, would overtake the rosebush, would shade my head in the summer—outside reading Mayakovsky—and would prevent the neighbor's loose branch hanging over my yard from crushing my back porch? I didn't know. He did. Not like a fortune teller with tricks. Not like a prince with a magic mirror foreseeing my demise, no, like an experienced farmer who plants everywhere during a drought, a famine, with a hope something will take.

HORROR MOVIE

Sure, it starts with a couple sipping an iced caramel macchiato at a
coffeeshop, cuddling on the couch munching popcorn, and slow dancing
to an upbeat song at the club. One asks a question. If the answer is yes, the
reward is a blood diamond or another useless rock. Then, flowers, vows,
hugs from family, kiss, lotto numbers. Throw a penny in the fountain—
make a wish. Hell, make it a 50-cent piece. Honeymoon, if you're lucky,
mortgage if you like debt and repairs and neighbor dogs barking at six
in the morning. You forgot to put out your trash cans last night and the
garbage truck has already passed by, and the hall light's burned out—you
stub your toe. *O Fortuna* begins. Now all the lights go out, the phones, not
charged, remain black, and something enters—perhaps through an open
window, or stuck on the bottom of a shoe, or attached to the junk mail piled
on the dining room table. It spreads through the vents, but its odor cannot
be detected. You purchase a radon test kit. Everyone has secrets. The first
time it appears you make excuses, and it vanishes. The next time it hovers
overhead while you cuss. The tension builds as the score ends and now one
lone violin purrs and eventually squeals. Your eyes adjust. It's everywhere.
Wanted children never arrive or leave too soon while the unwanted multiply.
The affair was always there—you were naïve. The bruises, broken promises,
and broken ribs are all one has to give. The bills explode your wallet and
mailbox. The cancer, diabetes, lower back pain and heart attack are waiting
out back behind the shed. You open the front door, stand naked beneath
the stars, and imagine another house, another marriage. But that's the bitch
of it—the monster is fair. Something must happen everywhere. So you turn
off the movie before it strikes again, but the reel continues to spin. Despite
never having read the script, you know the lines and you make it to the end.

TO GET TO THE OTHER SIDE

The long Iowa road winds like the one
rolling on in that Beatles' song.
Even though it was out of the way, I would
never miss the chance to drive you home.
The high beams flash, so deer dart and
maneuver like shadows. The green hills
invisible in darkness beckon the deer,
"Come here! Come here!" Each trip I would comment
how their suicidal tendencies didn't make sense,
and once you played devil's advocate:
everyone risks his life in love.
Love. A tourniquet on the conversation.
What did we know of it? As if you
and I had ever felt the maddening
lure of anyone. Yet I had. I would
travel anywhere to be near you.
Even if semis and SUVs and cars
raced between us, I'd venture forward.
See. Why did the deer cross the road?

MESSAGES

We text back and forth—volleying *hello,*
how are you?, are you okay?, hang in there,
and we promise to get together someday
in the distant future when we will sit side
by side at a table in a Cold Stone Creamery
and pass our poems back and forth—
a tennis match—our pens such sturdy rackets,
the subject a ball, filled with feathers stitched
with thread, we could never serve over
the net. In such an open stance,
feet parallel to the door, torso coiled
like a snake ready to strike, I always lose
my balance. I'm wobbly and small
like that table waiting for us. Your
calf steadies the table leg to keep
it from teetering. One foot, closer to the exit,
the other ahead, the neutral stance
allows you to shift your weight,
maintain your composure. Do you
remember that Coke bottle I purchased
just because it had my ex's name on it?
Remember that giant milkshake
with that giant straw? Remember how you
made me laugh until I cried? No, you don't
because it hasn't happened, and we
are trapped, separate, and the score
remains love-love.

to deboard before the launch
and for keeping the exit open.
With its red sign sting
and robotic voice count-
down 10-9-8-7,
the flight seemed inevitable
and I wouldn't have left
without prodding, without
my luggage that you
kindly carried to the tarmac.
Once you were out of sight,
the thundering echo of engines
silenced, the stars fell
from the sky and like a giant
page of connect-the-dots
they formed lines—my name
burnt into a Nebraska cornfield
hundreds of miles away.
I bloomed again (how many
times can one bloom?).
Now I'm old enough
to know all harvests end
and most rockets—raging
into the night sky—don't follow
strict flight plans, and never
return to where they first soared,
instead, they plunge to the ocean
with chute open and a rescue
boat waiting to pull the crew
aboard. I never learned to swim
and I won't be there to carry
you back to shore. I stay home
here in the corn—the sky
is open and my neck,
no longer sore.

MY FRIEND AND I VISIT HOLLYWOOD CANDY AT 8:55PM ON A TUESDAY

After a couple of drinks at the poetry reading,
after we buy copies of the books and get them signed,
we head to the ice cream parlor, but ice cream
isn't my treat. The candy store—with its walls
of candy cigarettes that leave chalk outlines
on lips and fingertips (years ago my friends
and I pretended to be adults dragging on a smoke,
tapping ash onto the sidewalks)—calls my name
and look, the "open" neon sign blazes—the red
torch to light the way. We jaywalk. I pull
on the door, but it won't budge. You give
it a try, too, but no, it's locked. Peering into
the shop window, there is the Coca Cola polar bear,
eight feet tall, with his eyes darting back and forth,
the 50s style counter with the old-fashioned register
that rings each time the drawer opens,
huge suckers the size of baby heads,
swirls of rainbows on sticks in a cracked glass jar.
All this sugar waits behind the glass. An employee
walks past but won't make eye contact.
Two kids still shopping disappear down
an aisle filled with taffy and gum. I pound
on the window expecting someone to come,
but no one does. I'm locked out.
What have I done? I throw up my hands
in defeat. The laughter starts.
Now I can't speak, tears rolling down
my cheeks. "Look at the sign—they don't close
until nine. They won't let us in! They see us!"
I gasp. And you, with your ice cream cone, nod,
but I don't think you get it. Not at all.
Until two days later you arrive
at my office with a couple of boxes
of candy cigarettes, and the thought
of those people behind the glass hoarding
all those sweets tickles me again.
I thank you for the cigarettes and slip
one between my teeth. Months later
I won't mention that the night of forbidden
candy stays with me—a sugar rush every time.

NOVEMBER

For your birthday

Did you know that all November-born
people have nine lives?
Every occupation, educational pursuit,
embrace lasting longer than thirty seconds,
sheds the skin—you are
revised, re-clothed, reborn clutching
a library card bearing your new name.
Years ago, I thought of men as scorpions.
With venom, they paralyze victims.

Their pincers pinch, stingers pulsate,
and then they retreat as quick as a snap
of a claw, a flick of a tail.
Did you know that I have nine lives
despite my birth in February?
In each episode, I was stung
by a skittering shadow
hiding beneath a rock or weed,
but with you, I pranced

along in this tank top and skirt
and remained safe.
For a time, this stung
worse than other encounters.
Here in the rocky field, I study
the sky, and invite you to relax
on the stone beside me. The sunset,
with its topaz hue—Kansas fires
in the distant—eventually

disappears leaving the sky
black. Examine the stars. See
how Orion escapes
to hide from the danger
of the scorpion's claws. The signs
rise separately. See how I leave
myself open, a notebook with its pages
flapping in the evening breeze,
and how each scribbled word

is a plea. Note that
our words, like stars,
are constellations and if you
direct your attention to the west,
I'm adding your name to mine—
calculating nine times nine
times nine times nine. Every
equation needs an antidote,
a penultimate word from a friend.

REFLECTION ON THE FINAL YEAR

As you drag the shovel, it screeches along
the rocks. The moss grows—sticky and wet—
across your sweaty face and hangs to your chin.
The sloth, latched to your neck, piggybacks
the entire journey, increasing in weight
with every step. If you knew the miles left
to the site, you'd pick up the pace, but you
don't, so move as a glacier did—inches
across the continent—all those years ago.

SPACE MAKES

fingers numb, blue, and pruned

a moon spin away in disgust

icy flowers bloom inside clouds

a bent knee a proposal

rippled flags fall over

a distant wave an obscene gesture

THE FIRST MEETING

Caffeine Dreams—rickety chairs, wobbly tables,
70s-era sofas stained with spilled coffee
and sticky with pastry crumbs, the grinding roar
behind the counter, the clink and scratch
of spoons and mugs, a too-tight staircase
to the backdoor, an outdoor patio, maze-like
in its arrangement of lopsided tables and mismatched
stools, and two or three gathering spots hidden
by tree branches and vines—is a coffeeshop
with ample parking but no indoor space
to maneuver. A person with any girth will
knock over someone's laptop or drink
or end up in a lap if her shoe catches
the broken linoleum. I tripped that day
when you arrived late. You showed off
your huge calves with those red short shorts.
I was sure you were a professor
from a different university: your words
were so confident, your interruptions
so numerous. I didn't know then
about white male privilege or
that some things you said were sexist.
I assumed I was uneducated. Distracted
by your legs, I bounced my eyes
around the room. Reclining
on that lumpy couch, I wished I could stay
the whole day to listen to your witty
remarks. When the group dispersed,
you held back. You didn't back
down when we disagreed on Plath.
When the coffeeshop closed,
we chatted in the parking lot,
and I hoped at the next meeting you'd
come again in those red shorts.

SHOPPING AT TARGET WITH MY ~~EX LOVER~~ FRIEND

You say you need to find an ointment that your father asked for, so we're
in the pharmacy department: shelves full of pain relief, allergy relief, gas
relief, dietary supplements. Last year I heard that big brand companies
pay more for eye-level shelf space; someone had studied how we shop,
and then schemed and plotted for that cough syrup and nose spray's spot.
You're searching the shelves closest to the floor, and I keep getting in the
way. The aisles are crowded with carts and gray-haired ladies—*excuse me*—
so I wander to the end-cap filled with bandages and Neosporin. I select
the pink and white polka dot no-name band-aid box and return to your
side to put it in the cart. You raise an eyebrow. *For my daughter,* I answer,
and throw in kid sunscreen—not the expensive kind with the baby's
diaper falling off—lotion that's thick and blinding white and probably
expires before the end of summer. After finding what your father needs,
we stroll to the groceries. Again, you're looking for a sale—cans of
chili and soup—and I'm eyeing the refried beans with the green label
"Vegetarian." In the next aisle, I drop a plastic sleeve of gum and a box
of gumdrops next to the sunscreen. My items take up most of the cart,
for you have placed yours next to the handlebar where a baby would sit,
where my purse would normally rest. We go down every aisle with you
pushing those squeaky wheels, and after an hour, we head to the registers.
We both dislike self-checkout so we wait. At the conveyor belt, you place
everything together—unsorted—and insist on paying for my items along
with yours. I've learned not to argue when a man says he's paying, but I
say thank you five times, and outside I watch as you put the cart back in
the corral, rebag, and make sure your items are in their own sack. You
carry everything, including my 24-case of Diet Pepsi. We load up my
trunk and then yours. You ask if I want to grab a bite to eat, and I say, *let
me pay.* Now we're in a Dairy Queen booth. You slurp a milkshake, using
the straw as a spoon, and I munch on hot French fries and chicken strips.
As we shopped, we discussed your father's health condition, my discipline
challenges with the kids, and American consumerism, but now I ask about
the past. Why did you respond to that desperate email a dozen years ago
when you were six hours away by car and un-tethered to Omaha? Back

then, we hadn't spoken in six months when I sent you that note: I was getting a divorce, my husband arrested, my skin bruised. I expect you to say that you had loved me all along, a city bench at that Dodge Street bus stop that sits undeterred through snow, ice, and wind, waiting for the thaw and all those commuters to return in the spring. You say, *pity*. You say, *friend*. I wonder if everything has been done out of pity for I am a pitiful creature who has spent years wandering grocery stores and malls hunting for the best deal, only to fall victim to my flat feet. I want to ask what kind of pity makes a man put his hands down a woman's pants, finger her till she comes, over and over. But I don't. Perhaps it's pride that lifts my head, puts a smile on my face while I nod as if I have known all along that you, with that straw hanging out of your mouth, never intended to take me home. I've been left alone to spoil.

NEW YEAR'S EVE MESSAGE

I want to send this before midnight,
but my internet's been cutting in and out.
The router and modem blink red and white—
little sparks and flickers—a Christmas
tree beneath my desk. My office is lit up
like an alien spaceship—the glow
and jerking light on the dashboard
of a doomed flight. I'm not a luddite—
I restart, unplug, push the reset button,
but every email to you goes unsent.

Non-violent communication—now called
compassionate communication—I studied
during marriage counseling with my ex.
Those techniques didn't work then, or now.
Our attempts at poetry, love, and space
exploration failed. Oh well. I hope you're next
to a fireplace holding someone close,
ignoring the computer and phone, sipping
on hot chocolate with marshmallows.
I can't return. I trip on wires, things go blast,
and my responses are never opened.

Maybe my emails have been abducted. You too.
Dozens of men—frozen in vats—stand
in a lab awaiting release. The good news:
I don't see you there. We weren't serious
enough to morph into monster. I want to be
the one who got away, but that's not true.
We are friends. I wish I could erase the rest.
If I did that, there would be no poems, no book.
No, I want to write you.

We have the same keyboard, all letters
in the same order, the same cursor—
the black line pulsating like the burn
on the eye after the camera's flash,
a blinking yield sign at the train tracks,
the heart monitor reporting the body's rhythm,
and the same 20-weight, standard bright
multipurpose paper (for everyday performance),
and the same brand printer that jams
when fed too much at once, yet we arrive
to the table with such different takes.
I'm one-syllable words—dark, breast, rope,
kiss, drench, quench. Your diction's higher
and you never get undressed. I guess art
does replicate life. I hit send. You hit delete.

AFTER PLAYING MINECRAFT FOR THE FIRST TIME, I REFLECT ON LOVE

Tunneling through rock and dirt,
I create a maze, a temple,
a hidden world. I invite
you inside, but you
refuse—I've no blueprints,
maps, nor explanation
as to why I've spent
years underground—
my nails chipped, my skin
pale, my vocabulary
limited to earth, wall,
water, and turnaround.
I can't describe the urge
to crawl on my knees
in darkness and mud,
flicking insects off my face,
to find the perfect cave
where bats screech
and the stench purges
hunger and thirst,
where the only light
filters through the small
entrance, and how romantic
this all is—to build
my own home away
from eyes and expectations.
I accept your refusal
and hunt again. This
time for a mate who
is not preoccupied
with square house design
and manicured lawns,

who understands all
journeys in love require
work and dirt, who
will wipe my brow
at the end of a long day
and continue the dig
when I'm too weak to ask
for help, when I'm too shy
to admit I've lost the way.

SPECIAL THANKS

A warm thank you to all the editors for giving my poems such good homes. It's been an honor to be in your pages and on your sites.

A special thank you to my writing group: Katie Berger, Annemarie Burton, Sky Dixon, Fran Higgins, Michelle Lyles, and Clif Mason.

A thank you to TMW for being my friend and mentor and for having the courage to embark on this journey together even though we ended up writing separate.

A heartfelt thank you to Rachel Brodsky for the beautiful artwork on the cover.

An immense thank you to Susan Aizenberg, Alvin Greenberg, and Diana Goetsch.

A thank you to the band Orchestral Manoeuvres in the Dark for creating a song that has stayed with me for decades. The titles of the sections in this book come from the song "If You Leave."

This collection is dedicated to Leonard Cohen. He is the reason I write.

ABOUT THE AUTHOR

Cat Dixon is the author of *Eva* and *Too Heavy to Carry* (Stephen F. Austin University Press, 2016 and 2014) and *The Book of Levinson* and *Our End Has Brought the Spring* (Finishing Line Press, 2017 and 2015), and the chapbook, *Table for Two* (Poet's Haven, 2019). Cat is a poetry editor with *The Good Life Review* and an adjunct instructor at the University of Nebraska, Omaha. Her poetry and reviews have appeared in numerous journals. She was the co-editor of *Watching the Perseids: The Backwaters Press Twentieth Anniversary Anthology* (BWP, 2017). She lives in Nebraska with her children, Pierce and Leven.

CPSIA information can be obtained
at www.ICGtesting.com
Printed in the USA
BVHW042151181022
649665BV00004B/17